BÔ YIN RÂ
(JOSEPH ANTON SCHNEIDERFRANKEN)

ENIGMAS
OF NATURE'S
INVISIBLE REALM

For information about the books of Bô Yin Râ and
titles available in English translation
visit The Kober Press web site at
http://www.kober.com

BÔ YIN RÂ
(JOSEPH ANTON SCHNEIDERFRANKEN)

ENIGMAS
OF NATURE'S
INVISIBLE REALM

TRANSLATED FROM THE GERMAN BY
JAN SCHYMURA, MALKA WEITMAN
AND ERIC STRAUSS

THE
KOBER
PRESS

BERKELEY, CALIFORNIA

For permission to quote or excerpt, email:
koberpress@mindspring.com

This book is a translation from the German of
Okkulte Rätsel, by Bô Yin Râ (J.A. Schneiderfranken),
published in 1923 by Verlag Magische Blätter,
Leipzig, Germany. The copyright to the German text
is held by Kober Verlag, AG, Bern, Switzerland.

Printed in the United States of America

International Standard Book Number: 978-0-915034-21-5

Typography and composition by Dickie Magidoff

Book cover after a design by Bô Yin Râ

CONTENTS

PREFACE

ONLY ONE THING IS IMPORTANT! ALL my writings seek to point out this "one thing" and all my efforts try to show how to attain it safely.

If, however, I speak of things in this book that are of a totally different nature, it is to shed more light on the path to that one thing and keep readers from straying onto needless byways.

THOSE WHO RESOLVE to climb the steep ascent leading to the Spirit's luminous heights need help right from the outset lest they lose sight of their goal.

Their path starts in daily life and leads, only gradually, higher and higher, so that it may take some time until they find themselves at last suffused by the clear, living light of pure, spiritual Being. Before arriving at this goal, other rays of light will attract their gaze and try to gain their interest. Those who seek to find their way must learn to recognize the nature of these earthly lights so that they will not be deceived.

But not all light emanating from this planet is deceptive.

Indeed, various kinds of radiances, whose glow emanates from invisible terrestrial regions, may offer help on the path towards the Spirit, if the seeker knows how to use them in the right manner. This is because, while they are alive, seekers are still subject to the bonds of their physical bodies—still subject to laws originating from the same primordial womb of physical Being that has and always will determine the inherent nature and effect of these earthly lights.

"Have dominion over the earth and subdue it!"

Not by disregarding its hidden powers do humans become masters of the earth but, rather, through knowledge of the laws to which everything terrestrial must bow and through knowledge of their own spiritual might, which can command everything that fills terrestrial space. Human beings have power to the same degree that their inner power is aligned with the eternal, ruling force that is the source of all existence.

In this book I will touch on things that one does not absolutely need to know in order to attain the highest spiritual goal, that is, the unification of our own consciousness with the Spirit of our timeless essence—the birth of the Living God in one's own soul.

However, these matters can become an obstacle for those who seek their timeless essence, or, on the other hand, may be a help to them in their ascent. Because of the lack of clarity surrounding the origins of the phenomena to be discussed, many seekers may find themselves in conflict: they cannot rationally integrate these things into their concept of reality and yet, these phenomena clearly make their influence felt in daily life so as to leave no doubt that they exist. It only can be beneficial for all aspiring to spiritual light if these phenomena are traced back to their roots and their true origins made plain.

Out of ignorance many people equate hidden science with superstition, without suspecting that when one fails to distinguish between the two, the harmless weeds of superstition, but also the very poisonous ones, find fertile soil upon which they can flourish, depriving nobler plants of their strength and stunting their growth.

There is no better way to uproot superstitious interpretations from their soil than by laying bare the nature of these little-studied forces, so that their true nature can be recognized.

It will then become evident that in a time long before recorded history began, humanity was in some ways wiser than the present age, so proud of its "progress" and "enlightenment."

Many a finding from former times that was thoughtlessly considered to be superstition is now considered to be based on fact. Yet there is much more to discover in order to permanently free hidden science from superstitious delusion, and thus allow many secrets of nature that are hidden from our sense perception, to serve humanity anew.

One needs to approach the subject matter before us without the shackles of prejudice, to find what can be found, and to learn to separate the worthless and misleading from the valuable and true.

Above all, it is important to test these matters for one's self before one is entitled to make a judgment.

Preconceived ideas and opinions, even when supposedly directed against superstition, have always provided the breeding ground where superstition hides and grows unchecked.

Not by trying to avoid all darkness does one demonstrate fearlessness but, rather, by being able to calmly walk through the darkness, acting firmly whenever apparitions attempt to scare.

THERE ARE OTHER REASONS why I felt it necessary to write this book. Many areas that we will cover have for quite some time been the province of dilettantes as well as serious investigators.

A vast quantity of books varying in degrees of quality deal with the phenomena examined in the following chapters.

Many searching earnestly to find the path towards the world of radiant Spirit now suddenly find themselves confronted with these writings, and all too often believe themselves to have come face to face with revelations about spiritual worlds, unaware that in reality they are stumbling onto a path diametrically opposed to their original aspiration.

Others are afraid of any involvement with such things and live in foolish fear of the imagined "injury" they might receive from these realms.

This book was written to help eliminate both of these errors.

WHENEVER SEEKERS BELIEVE that the mysterious effects of hidden, terrestrial forces are manifestations of the highest regions of the Spirit, they may be led onto a false path that ends in a disastrous reversal of their intended course. On the other hand, if they fail to inform themselves about the nature and origin of these forces, held back by a thousand fears and believing only harm could come from these realms, they stand in their own way. Instead, they should master these forces so that they can be used as servants, thereby making it easier to walk the path that leads towards a sun no mortal eye has ever beheld, a sun that can only be perceived with spiritual organs in those regions of purest spirit that can be accessed only in one's innermost soul.

As mysterious as the matters this book attempts to shed light on may appear, without exception they do not lead to the realms of Spirit but, rather, still pertain to the external world, albeit to that much more expansive, external world that is difficult to apprehend since it is not accessible to the earthly senses.

Just as those who seek to find the Living Spirit must learn to master everything in the limited sphere of the external world that their mortal senses can perceive, so they must also learn to rule in the invisible region of the physical realm, that is accessible only through feeling, lest they be ruled by those very forces they have not recognized.

However, this does not mean that every person aspiring towards the Spirit needs first to investigate the magic forces of the earth.

They should simply know that if they encounter any of these forces on their path, they may use them as servants of their will to reach the spirit's heights, but must never let these forces make servants of them.

Such seekers may be likened to artists who, impelled by their creative impulse, do not hesitate to use whatever opportunities present themselves to further their artistic vision.

I trust I have sufficiently explained what has moved me to write this book.

May it provide the needed signposts to safely guide seekers to always find the way back to their upward-leading path, though they will encounter much on earthly roads that is also quite wondrous.

Capri, May 1922
Bô Yin Râ

CHAPTER ONE

SECRET KNOWLEDGE
AND
HIDDEN SCIENCE

T RULY, THERE EXISTS SECRET KNOWLEDGE, experienced by only a few, and despite all their persistent efforts, unattainable by those to whom it will not give itself.

Only the implications for the individual that flower from the source of this knowledge may be communicated so that in this way some seekers, although not knowing, but guided by an intuition rooted in the Source of All Knowing, may find their way towards the Spirit.

Having thus reached their highest goal, true knowledge may then become theirs.

Few are the born guardians and duty-bound servants of this knowledge, yet countless seekers from every generation have been guided by these few, at first towards an awakening knowledge of the path, then onto the path, and finally towards beholding knowledge itself.

Who would be so simple as to think that this knowledge is the same as certainty resulting from the human need to investigate; from that discipline of thought used to analyze terrestrial experience and commonly referred to as science?

Yet, there always have been scatterbrains and vain drivellers who try to impress the people of their time by pretending to have acquired the most secret spiritual knowledge, and to have made it into a "science," in imitation of the sciences of this earth, structured according to system and rule in order to "teach" it to their students.

With respect to such mystagogues, it probably is not too harsh a judgment to surmise that neither reverence for the knowledge that the Spirit of Eternity alone can give lives in them, nor that they approach with honor and respect what thinkers of all ages have discovered in the realms of science.

Those who have even once been touched in the depths of their souls by the radiance emanating from one of these two luminous sources of human knowledge would certainly only approach the other with appreciative reverence and never mistake the color of one for the color of the other.

Quite distinguishable is the Light of Terrestrial Reason, even if owing its radiance to exalted intuition, from the Light of Eternity, which can neither be deduced nor verified nor arrived at by thought and only reveals its existence to those who have attained it within their own Being.

One thing is "Secret Knowledge" and another "Hidden Science."

From every possible perspective I try to bring to seekers of my time word of that secret knowledge, and if today I also inform about hidden science, albeit providing only a framework for understanding rather than describing it in detail, let it be known right from the start that I only intend to bring clarification and by no means to present the results of scientific investigation.

In truth, apart from commonly known science, there also exists hidden science. Indeed, I could say that all science that is recognized nowadays, was once hidden.

Whoever is willing to consider the results of the past one hundred years of human investigation and thought will surely come to the same conclusion.

There also exists science that, once well known, was forced to retreat into obscurity. Senseless superstition had infiltrated it so thoroughly and threatened to overwhelm it, that it is a wonder it nevertheless succeeded in freeing itself.

One such science striving to become accepted once more is that discipline we call "astrology," which is gaining the respect of those who come to know it more closely.

I see here the resurrection of a science that has given support and security to the most enlightened spirits of bygone times. Although I do not feel myself called upon to become its disciple, and to advance this science from that position, I nevertheless know its most hidden laws and know, from spiritual knowledge, how to make use of them. I am able to truly value whatever is of value here.

MANY WHO READ these words will now raise the objection that it is wholly inappropriate to speak of the ancient art of interpreting the stars, which is experiencing a revival in our day, as a science.

They will refer to the countless charlatans whose advertisements fill the columns of newspapers and consider it to be beneath their dignity when I speak of astrology as a science.

When I look at those newspaper columns I not only note the advertisements of so-called astrologers, but also, in even greater number, the proclamations of so-called doctors, of people referring to themselves as skilled in the art of healing.

Would it not be foolish, just because of these advertisements, to deny all medical art its scientific base?

In both cases there exists a real skill, arduously acquired, based on real science.

In both cases there exists an ordered system whose structure has been shaped by the most enlightened thinkers of past ages.

In both cases, all intellectual knowledge and all experience gained will not lead to anything unless inspired intuition guides, case by case, the way in which science should be applied in everyday practice.

In both cases, finally, there exist, apart from those persons with a scientific conscience, also charlatans without conscience who, at best, believe themselves to stand far above science. In most cases, however, they belong to that unscrupulous sort who lives off the unteachability of certain people—especially those who are suspicious of rational thinking, even in situations where rational thought is the obvious approach, because, alas, their attempts have usually ended in fiasco.

However, I have compared the science of astrology and the science of medicine not only for their apparent similarities but also for deeper reasons.

Medicine too has not always been the way we know it today. Nowadays it too is in the process of evolving so that even its most experienced representatives, whose scholarliness is irrefutable, find themselves, more often than they would like, face to face with enigmas. Medicine too has its store of knowledge and skills that can be learned and yet all this knowledge and skill does not make a good doctor.

In astrology, just as in the medical arts, it is ultimately the personal aptitude of those who dedicate themselves to either of these two sciences that is the determining factor. Never will unsuited persons be able to fully realize all the possibilities in their chosen field.

I can well understand that today people are inclined to speak of astrology as a science that is still evolving. My own understanding, however, bids me to caution those who lack actual knowledge of the subject not to deny true astrological investigation its scientific base.

Granted that some of those investigating in this field may fall short of the educational standards of today. They reveal their educational gaps especially when they naively believe they must make use of scholarly-sounding jargon in their writings instead of using the language to which they are accustomed.

Granted too that today the traditional language of astrology may appear antiquated, even crude or superstitious.

But what on earth have these deficiencies got to do with the real core of the matter, with the investigation of the way in which astrological forces influence our lives?

Sick people will surely not reject a doctor who they believe can heal them just because they notice that this expert has inclinations different from them in other areas.

The person who would arrive at a sound verdict regarding astrology is best advised to calmly overlook everything that is extraneous to the core of the matter, and to pay attention only to the findings that can be arrived at by means of astrological investigation, findings that actually have been confirmed quite frequently. One should not consult charlatans but, rather, those who have a natural calling to this science, if one's horoscope is to serve as a guide for this life on earth. Such a horoscope is nothing other than what a meteorological chart is to the aviator.

It shows more or less accurately the possibilities for a particular individual's life span that can lead to either well-being or misfortune, teaches how to fight evil forces, and may prevent those individuals from standing in their own way. It provides a faithful analysis of the forces, good as well as bad, that form themselves around a human self, thus teaching its owner to bring order to the house of the soul.

It clearly indicates coming dangers that an attentive person may still evade, as well as showing one the favorable stations on the path through life.

A good horoscope can serve as a real blessing in one's life and only those who prefer to grope in the dark instead of having clear knowledge of their earth-given powers and the way in which they manifest themselves will be disquieted by its analysis.

To be sure, proper instruction is needed so that individuals do not hold a narrowly fatalistic view of their horoscope as some sort of inescapable destiny.

A horoscope will only be of real help when it rouses a person's will to avoid that which, according to its prediction, is most threatening unless, through counteraction, the potentially damaging force is broken.

A MAJOR OBSTACLE to the recognition of astrological laws today, especially in our scientific age, is the old theory still serving to explain the effects of astrology.

At this point I would like to provide some clarifying remarks out of my own perception, although I am aware that a certain flexibility of mind on the part of astrological investigators will be required in order for them to be receptive.

I must explicitly state that I am not proposing some kind of new theory but rather describing real natural phenomena that are relevant here.

To those who came after, all astrological teachings that have come to us from bygone days seemed to be based on the assumption that the mysterious effects of the celestial bodies on a person's destiny are deciphered here. However, modern scientific thinking rightly refuses to accept a theory that allows such enormous influence to emanate from unimaginably distant heavenly bodies.

In those olden times too, many refused to accept such an assumption and attempted to explain observed phenomena by proposing that these heavenly bodies were only the physical carriers of tremendously potent spiritual forces. Aside from any physical effects, their purely spiritual irradiance was supposed to reach our earth and thus affect a person's destiny.

More recent developments in astrology, however, indicate that it is time to look for the real causes of the observed effects in a place where they are actually to be found and to assign the heavenly bodies from which these effects supposedly emanate, their proper place in astrological investigation.

We are dealing with nothing less than the realization that the position of the heavenly bodies is only of importance to the astrologer because it represents the one possible way of determining certain points of influence to be found within the earth's aura.

Strictly speaking, all astrological research bears a misleading name.

In reality, it is not a matter of investigating the nature of the heavenly bodies but, rather, a matter of investigations within the earth's aura. The position of the heavenly bodies must be considered because certain time sequences of auric energy flows can only be determined through the corresponding position of those bodies. This is because the inhabitants of the earth have no other measuring points available to them, except for the geometrically ordered images projected by the other celestial bodies of the cosmos.

The invisible aura of this earth not only surrounds, in multiple layers, the surface of this planet, but also penetrates it right through to its inmost core.

Now, certain energy currents emanate in rhythmic intervals from the innermost core of the planet, flowing from the inside to the outside and then returning back to the center, traversing all layers of the earth's aura, like ocean currents.

The rhythm of the sending out and drawing in of these currents is completely dependent on the position of the earth relative to the sun. This means that the sun is actually the only heavenly body influencing the course of terrestrial life and the destinies of the earth's inhabitants, also in the realm of the soul. The moon, as the sun's reflector, plays an important role in this. The currents of the earth's aura, determined by the sun, impact the psycho-physical life of human beings. It is these types of currents with which astrology is concerned.

The variety of the currents, ranging from parallel flow to extreme counteraction, as well as their manifold kinds of penetration, which may be likened to the delicate colored threads of Murano glass, permits a nearly countless number of different combinations. All human beings thus receive their fundamental disposition for life as a result of the combination present at the time and place each of them first beheld the light, even though they were also indirectly under the influence of such currents while inside their mother's womb right from the very first moment of conception. These prenatal currents too play a part in determining the final form of the person's fundamental disposition.

In every second of a person's life, the combinations of energy currents in the earth's aura interact with the currents that determined the basic form, manifesting unique relationships and thereby shaping that person's course of life in very different ways.

Popular thought traces the influence of the auric currents to the heavenly bodies that are observed at the same time. However, it is definitely not the stars that are responsible for the shaping of destiny. This notwithstanding the fact that many astrological investigators perceive a close connection between the energy currents of the earth's aura and a particular constellation of stars, and thus ascribe their effect to the stars themselves.

Age-old wisdom knew of the true connection, however, such insight was already erased long before recorded history began.

IT IS NEITHER my task nor my intention to provide conclusive proof for the unshakeable necessity of the process described above. Instead, I put my faith in those persons who consider their calling in life to be the scientific investigation of astrological relationships, trusting that they can, more readily than myself, furnish the necessary, tangible proof. Empirical evidence will serve as better proof than the most elegant cosmological line of reasoning.

Perhaps these explanations will motivate scientific investigators other than practicing astrologers to take an interest in the striking effects of those forces that enchain individuals as well as whole nations, until these forces are finally understood and can thus be put to use.

In this way an almost hidden science may become manifest once more and with it the reawakened understanding that human beings inhabiting this earth are able to care for their physical life, as well as for the life of their soul, only insofar as they learn to master the forces of this earth. The task here is to use the freedom thus gained to develop the self in alignment with one's highest aspirations.

❧

CHAPTER TWO

THE PLANET'S HELPING FORCES

THERE IS A GROWING REALIZATION IN OUR day that antiquity built on a firm foundation with regard to many things, even if today every detail cannot yet be verified by science, whereas recent generations, only too proud of the rightness of their own knowledge, looked upon these same things as dark superstition.

Many treasures remain to be retrieved here, but whoever would unearth them, besides acquiring the needed knowledge, must also have the courage, in the face of dominant theories of the day, to lay bare the encrusted fossils from ages past and show them as they once really were. However, even then, investigators will err significantly unless inspired intuition grant that they, in every case, arrive at the right interpretation where others would, at first glance, consider such a discovery as evidence of wild superstition.

Those who sincerely desire to come upon the trail of truth in these matters should take the very greatest care to separate that which has worth from that which has no worth.

Mountains of debris heaped up with pre-conceived opinions must first be cleared out of the way for them to gradually arrive at the place where others stood millennia ago.

How can they gain clarity until they stand where the ancients stood—the place that taught the ancients to see different things and to see differently than our present age with its completely changed perspective on the world?

In a way one needs to search for one's own ancestors and learn to understand the whis-perings of one's own blood. One needs to be receptive to the truth contained in long-forgotten myths and legends taking care not a priori to dismiss those teachings where modern science seems already to have found conclusive answers, only to decide differently once human minds no longer are held captive by prevailing theory.

No matter how highly we may value the results of earnest intellectual effort, experience shows us, day by day, that even apparently well-grounded conclusions are, by far, not so firmly anchored as to be able to withstand newer and better findings.

Who would here dare to say: "We have long investigated everything and whatever is beyond that can only harbor error!"

That which we consider to be sure knowledge supported by experience probably contains more error than the present age could possibly imagine. And those who believe today, sure of their knowledge, that they are justified in jeering at bygone times and their "superstitions," do not realize that precisely here, where we consider ourselves to be most "enlightened," is to be found superstition with the gravest consequences: namely, the superstition that the ancients, more than us, were only victims of their delusions, incapable of formulating through rational thought those simple arguments against their theories that any simpleton today is capable of coming up with, when unable to unravel the customs and practices of ancient times.

We would truly serve ourselves better to concede distant ages at least some capacity for logical thinking, all the more so since wise persons of those times took care to pay attention to things that modern science would label as superstitious.

AMONG THE BELIEFS our intellectual arrogance would have us think outdated is the faith of all peoples in particular precious stones capable of bringing fortune or misfortune, as well as the belief in the power of amulets and talismans to protect the carriers of such sacred objects from evil or to attract life's blessings to them.

Upon first glance it is quite understandable that people would assume they are facing misguided superstition here. It is also certain that actual superstition, at all places and times, has found a wide-open playground among these practices.

Nonetheless, the ancients were not quite as credulous as their distant grandchildren, enthralled by their own cleverness, are rashly inclined to believe.

The ancients knew, just as well as us, if not more so, how to distinguish between justified and well-founded belief and that which, quite rightly, is labeled as superstition.

The ancient sages too were not wont to thoughtlessly accept assertions which, lacking any logical explanation, could only be supported by conjecture and guesswork. Nonetheless, they knew of stones that could bring fortune or misfortune, of amulets and protective talismans.

It is true that the theory on which their explanation of effect and cause rested was determined and bound by a worldview that has long since been corrected. However, the fact that a given cause could be confirmed by a particular effect was amply demonstrated to them through experience, so that any who would be so blind as to call this superstition would, in their eyes, be regarded as ignorant and hopeless fools.

Any serious investigators who are free of prejudice will confirm that these ancients were not wrong, if they make the effort to verify for themselves and others to what extent the effects confirm that which antiquity has left behind about such things.

Those who are willing to make this effort are on the one right path and will have some singular and remarkable experiences here, even if they cannot accept all of the ancients' theories.

Soon they will be able to bear witness to the fact that we are dealing here with something other than superstition and with more than simply the result of one's own or someone else's suggestive influence.

Similar effects may very well result from the power of suggestion and it may certainly be granted that some effects ascribed to stones, talismans and amulets can clearly be proven to result from such suggestive influence. But then, there also exist persons who only imagine they are ill yet no one would, just because of this, deny the possibility of real diseases.

The occurrence of a pseudo-effect does not preclude the real effect.

It is rather a question of determining to what extent the real effect differs from the merely illusory.

Anyone who looks into this question even just a little can confirm that this difference is strikingly apparent.

Even in the present day, it is surely not only dreamers pursuing fantasies who apply themselves to studies of this sort.

Indeed, serious and sober observation, time-consuming and arduous labor, as well as clear and critical judgment are necessary if one would attain trustworthy results in this field that still today is viewed with much skepticism by the rigorous sciences. Many an error remains to be corrected, yet also, many a truth remains to be found that today is still considered superstition.

But then, how are the effects considered here, that appear so mysterious, finally to be explained?

There have always been, at any given time, quite different theories with respect to these effects, varying with the cultures involved. Nonetheless, all these effects derive in every case from purely physical relationships, even if the natural laws operating here have not been proven to the same extent as, for example, the laws of physics.

Every person, even if only somewhat observant of everyday life, will notice time and again, how more sensitive people who are not just concerned with purely monetary value when selecting a piece of jewelry, no matter how modest, will typically show preference for particular types of gemstones.

Already apparent here is the effect of planetary law, even if the persons choosing are not conscious of it and follow only their own personal feelings. These relationships were once clearly evident to the wisdom of long past ages and more recent efforts seek to fathom them anew.

We are dealing here with nothing other than the infinitely varied energy currents of the earth's aura about which I have previously spoken in my comments regarding the value of astrology.

There I pointed out that all human beings on this globe receive an imprint of certain combinations of such energy currents, according to the constellation of earth forces that existed at the moment of their birth. This imprint affects all human beings' further experiences in such a way as to cause them to react in a particular manner, so that the myriad combinations of earth forces they encounter in every second of their earthly life take active shape in interaction with the original imprint.

Now, all things on this planet stand in relationship to the earth's energy currents. This relationship is richly abundant in the world of crystal forms, especially in gemstones, held in high esteem since ancient times.

Plants and animals as well as all metals are similarly determined by these energy currents.

In these cases, too, what we call "preferences" are nothing more than the intuitive sensing of relationships governed by natural laws.

Not only because of its rarity has gold been accorded the status of a fundamental worth, since the most ancient times and by all peoples on earth who knew of its existence.

Narrow-minded theoreticians with well-meaning intentions have thought up all sorts of theories in order to, once and for all, divest gold of its power and worth, because they believe to have found in it the source of all misfortune on this planet.

I certainly do not question the concern for humanity in their efforts, still, I have good reasons to doubt that these reformers know what they are doing.

Thankfully, these laws rest on firmer foundations than all such theory, so that gold will always be able to assert its worth even when the last traces of these theories have been extinguished in a new epoch of human endeavor. No theory, as plausible as it may sound, will ever be able to refute the fact that any nation that severs all links between gold and its currency, will lose its real prosperity—even if it has vast quantities of gold locked in its coffers.

If a nation is to truly blossom and not just stagnate, gold must circulate from hand to hand and be worn as jewelry, even in less affluent circles, its wearers thus participating in its circulation.

This circulation must take place in the form of material gold, because the circulation of paper money alone, even when abundantly backed by gold, cannot replace it.

It is a grave mistake to suspend the circulation of material gold, and this mistake will under all circumstances avenge itself bitterly, even if one believes that worse calamity will be averted in this way.

Affluence and life energy will be severely compromised in equal measure when every form of gold is withdrawn from circulation, even if done with best intentions, should this draining of gold from daily life last too long.

These are iron laws that even the strongest may not dare to challenge.

The reader who understands this entire chapter will also understand why I have here, apparently deviating from my subject, spoken of the significance of gold based on physical laws.

LET US NOW CONTINUE to consider the hidden influences on the individual person, even though a nation is ultimately no more than a collection of many individuals.

In the first of the books that I was allowed to give humanity in my days on earth, I made mention of "talismans," among other things.

(In English: *The Book On The Living God*, chapter 21, The Kober Press)

There, I very clearly explained how any object may be transformed into a talisman, as soon as it is willed, by an act of the faith that can move mountains, to bring good fortune to its bearer.

One may equally speak of talismans for bringing evil, since not only the morally upright are capable of creating a talisman in this way. Should such people wish another ill, they can, with the same confidence and faith, imbue an object of their choosing with destructive energy, and can "charge" that object with their will to bring upon its bearer every evil.

And now, I wish to speak of a different kind of talisman.

There also exist talismans that can only be created by those knowledgeable about the laws to which I have already alluded—talismans whose preparation require painstaking labor and extensive study. Similarly, there exist amulets that receive their protective power not only from the human will but because, in them, the energy currents of the earth's aura find possibilities for manifesting, which can only be brought about in accordance with certain strictly-determined laws.

Only someone familiar with every aspect of these energy currents and their tides may be considered competent to be their creator.

Much fraud is perpetrated in such things, however, this does not negate the fact that all fakery aims to imitate for naive souls that which is authentic. It follows that the real thing must exist, as imitation only attempts to usurp the place of that which is authentic.

Whoever is unable here to distinguish true from false deserves to be deceived.

Those who still lack knowledge of such matters should become aware that the effects of these auric energy currents, flowing through the earth at all times, can at determined points in time and with certain precautionary measures be magnetically tied to particular symbols, particular metals or other objects, so that the bearer of such an object now possesses an accumulator of the forces that become activated through these auric currents at specific times.

Those who are unable to accept that such things are real may want to consider what only a century ago a physicist would have said about the possibility of producing luminous images of the inner structure of the living human body or of the possibility of sending messages through the air waves around the world—even though such possibilities would certainly not have been anything new to a small group of human beings on this planet, because these few are alive in the Spirit's realm, which encompasses everything possible in the physical realm, and the physical world only reflects what is possible in the Spirit's domain.

ONE SHOULD NOT in any way believe that the use of amulets, talismans or those gemstones that resonate harmonically with one's own earthly auric vibratory frequency could be considered wrong when viewed from a higher spiritual perspective.

One might just as well suppose that owning a good heater in wintertime is proscribed.

When considering real amulets, talismans and genuine gemstones, we are simply dealing with appropriate means, well proven through thousands of years, of harnessing the power of certain planetary helping forces for our life here on earth.

Those able to harness the power of such forces for themselves, whether as a result of their own expertise or by making use of someone else's knowledge, will always be at an advantage, just like those who make use of the material aids available on earth.

We are not dealing here with some sort of fantastic magical power and even less so with purely spiritual forces.

We are merely dealing with the physical forces of this planet that are invisible, yet able to be sensed, and whose power may be harnessed in this way.

Foolish are those who do not use such help to lighten the burdens of this life—be it that they refuse to believe in the existence of such helping forces, or are unwilling to heed the few guidelines necessary for their mastery.

All things terrestrial can serve the spiritual and everything temporal can serve the eternal if they are used in the right manner. Those, however, who, with an air of smug self-assurance, pass unseeing by all that nature provides as help should not be surprised when obstacle after obstacle confronts them. Nor have they cause for complaint, since they, themselves, mock every opportunity for help.

Wise people of all ages also knew how to harness the earth's forces for their spiritual well-being.

Only arrogant fools scoff at what they do not know.

WE ARE ENTERING a new age in which the wheat shall be separated from the chaff with inexorable justice. Ancient wisdom, still dishonored and disdained in our time, will in coming days celebrate its resurrection, while much that we have long regarded as well proven will lose its unquestioned authority.

The science of the many has always at one time been the knowledge of the few.

Physical laws intended to explain certain effects have always been formulated only after the effects had long since been recognized.

Those who would wait until all the world gives its "yea and amen" to the truth of something will have to content themselves with less for a long time, while others, who know how to seek and find, enjoy the benefits of their advantage.

Many things have at first been decried as superstition, and then much later, beyond all expectation, proven by science to be true.

Here before us lies a field in which sprout grains of many kinds, which all the weeds that have invaded over time cannot crowd out.

Those capable of harvesting here will not regret it!

Albrecht Dürer said: "Art lies hidden in nature; whoever can draw it out, has art!"

Similarly, a multiplicity of subtle forces lie hidden in nature awaiting those capable of using them.

The poorest person on earth here possesses unimagined riches.

If all those living on this earth would use the hidden power of which they are still unaware, much human misery would be eliminated.

However, before a force can be used, one must become familiar with it, or at the very least be able to believe in its existence.

Here too faith is the prerequisite for knowledge, and knowledge finds its confirmation only through experience.

Insofar as I appear to call for faith, it simply is because only faith makes such experience possible.

&

CHAPTER THREE

THE MYSTERY
OF DREAMS

AMONG THE MANY MILLIONS OF HUMAN beings living on this planet it would be hard to find anyone who has not had the experience of waking up with the memory of having gone through something that could not have taken place in the external world.

One remembers having been awake and fully conscious, in a world as real and tangible as the familiar world into which one has now awakened, yet no bridge can be found to connect the one world with the other.

In the waking world one is able to revisit places one had previously left, but here it is not possible to return at will to the world one has experienced.

Actions taken there leave no consequences in the waking world. Possessions owned there disappear without a trace. People with whom one may have just conversed have actually died long ago. Dangers that threatened there simply vanish on awakening.

There is only one quality this remembered world has in common with the waking world, that is, both seem equally real. But there is only one connection between both worlds that remains upon awakening, and that is the sense of one's own self—one's consciousness.

We refer to this strange experience, which does not require the use of our body and only leaves memories within, as a "dream," so as to distinguish it from the waking state.

Even in ancient times people were so impressed by these dream experiences, that they tried to penetrate their mystery.

Such dream experiences, in which one finds oneself awake, active and experiencing life, just as in the familiar, exterior world, while the physical body rests in profound sleep, were treated with reverential awe.

People searched for ways to make meaningful connections between dream experiences and the external world, often seeing the dreams as harbingers of coming events, and inventing a comprehensive vocabulary of symbols in order to connect the two.

Modern science also has pursued the path of dream interpretation. However, rather than looking to dreams to shed light on future events, today's investigators believe one can find in dreams the key to the dreamers' own strivings and aspirations as well as their most hidden desires.

W<small>HEN ONE CONSIDERS</small> both the old way as well as the new, strictly scientific way of interpreting dreams, one still must conclude that nothing of substance has been discovered about the miracle of dreaming itself.

Physiological research can at best only analyze the physical condition of the dreamer's body while dreaming and, therefore, theories based on it are not able to reveal the mystery of dreams. But dreams are nonetheless a most remarkable event, far beyond what psychological and physiological research can reveal, so it is worthwhile to consider the dreaming process in the light of purely spiritual cognition.

Our so-called "waking life" is influenced by our dreams more than most of us suspect.

It would not be an exaggeration to say that the experience of dreams has no less a share in the forming of character than one's experience in the outside world.

Even if one completely disregards one's dream remembrances or wakes up with only a vague memory of having dreamt, unable to lift the content of the dream into the light of consciousness, the dream experience will nevertheless have left its traces in the deepest, most hidden recesses of the brain's memory regions: in the cells of the ganglia, the storage batteries of the body's memory. In this way, dreams significantly influence the actions of our everyday lives, without us being aware of it.

Things come full circle here. Most dreams that have such a strong influence are likely determined by the thoughts, aspirations, inclinations, desires, and will of the dreamer, so that ultimately we reinforce our own thoughts and feelings while dreaming, and the dream is thus able to offer us valuable insights into ourselves.

Dreams can also bring welcome relief by giving dreamers the opportunity to have experiences that they would not allow themselves in everyday life. The dream allows them to release the inner tension created by the personality's pull towards such experiences, and the need to avoid them for ethical reasons.

Such dreams affect daily life not only by relieving inner tension but also, in most cases, by leaving the dreamers with a feeling akin to guilt, thus motivating them to strive even harder to live up to their personal, ethical standards. However, it is foolish, in such a case, to feel morally responsible for one's own dreams!

JUST AS THE EFFECTS of dreams on daily life are very different, so too are their causes.

Not everything that we refer to as a dream belongs to the realm of dreams alone.

A real dream, strictly speaking, consists of the perceptions of physical consciousness that take place within the body during sleep. This is a purely physiological process during which the body is cut off from full perception of the outside world and its laws that govern all earthly experience. During sleep such perceptions are only possible in the form of mental images created in the brain.

Impressions on the body from the outside world, no matter through which of the senses they may be felt are, without exception, perceived only in terms of their inner effect on the body, as if "seen" from the inside.

The sleeper feels the chill of the air around his or her bare foot while, in the body's cells, the memory of having once waded through cold water comes alive. At the same time the mental image of wading through a stream is created in the brain and, as a result, many other, related images are re-activated. These associated images are felt with more or less immediacy depending on how closely they are connected to the main mental image.

The presence of a diseased organ may stimulate mental images of an injury in the corresponding place in the dreamer's body, even if the disease has not yet produced symptoms during waking hours. Pressure on certain nerve pathways from food absorbed by the stomach and intestines, which may stimulate feelings of fear or anxiety during waking life, can during sleep lead to terrifying nightmares. These are all genuine and undiluted dream experiences according to my prior definition.

THE ABILITY TO DREAM, also possessed by animals, can be made use of from a dimension that, in itself, has nothing to do with dreams.

While the "real" dream only registers the effects of sensations taking place within the body's cells in the form of mental images, it is equally possible for a stirring of the soul forces, whose nature is completely non-physical, to try to influence the brain during sleep, just as they customarily do during waking hours.

However, the physiological changes that induce sleep insulate those points of contact from which the soul forces would otherwise be able to freely order the brain's activities. The soul forces can activate those mental images, latent in the brain, that are needed to communicate with the dreamer, but they are powerless with respect to other, peripheral images that are stimulated in the process.

The dream, activated from a dimension that, in itself, is quite distinct from dreaming, can present a very logically structured experience to the consciousness. It can also transform one experience into another in a kaleidoscopic manner, or present these experiences in an utterly chaotic way.

These types of dreams, which are not rooted purely in the physical realm, are now being explored in a scientific manner in order to gain deeper insights into the psyche of the dreamer, insights that can never be accessed through the dreamer's conscious mind during waking life.

This category includes the dreams of scholars who continue to pursue their research while dreaming, inventors who perfect their inventions while asleep, as well as artists who succeed in overcoming in the dream the artistic blocks that frustrate them during waking hours.

It also includes dreams that, when recalled upon awakening, actually present us with solutions to the most difficult challenges.

But these kinds of dreams ultimately bring nothing into the dreamer's awareness that has not already in some way been assimilated by the psyche and that, with the help of mental images stored in the brain, can be transformed into a dream experience.

THERE ALSO EXISTS a different kind of dreaming, and perhaps it was because of this kind that the dream was considered to be such a mystery by the ancients.

Just as the forces of the soul, both during waking hours and in sleep, are able to influence the brain cells, albeit in quite different ways, so too mental images of other entities—be they physically incarnated human beings; creatures inhabiting the invisible, physical realm; or sublime beings of the spirit's realm—can reach the brain of the sleeping or waking person. The brain's capacity for assimilation can be significantly greater during sleep than while awake, provided that the brain is not already busy with other kinds of dream experiences.

The dreams previously described were brought into being by the dreamer's own body cells or soul forces, whereas, in the dreams we are now discussing, individual, conscious beings separate from the dreamer step in, seeking to influence the dreamer through their own will and with conscious intention.

In these dreams a contact is established, with the brain acting as a transmitter between the dreamer and the outside agent. The information transmitted may vary greatly in value from seemingly neutral suggestions all the way to quasi-hypnotic orders. Profound spiritual counsel or insights may also be transmitted in this way.

Further, those who have departed from this earth are temporarily able, with the help of sublime, spiritual beings, to reach the consciousness of those still living in a physical body.

All prophetic dreams belong to this category, as well as all dreams of warning and deeply meaningful spiritual experiences during sleep that can be interpreted as help granted. However, in the same way malevolent influences too can make themselves heard and felt.

When recalling such dreams, dreamers must be able to evaluate their nature for themselves, a judgment that should not be difficult.

The more one is accustomed to acting in accordance with strict ethical guidelines in waking life, the easier it will be to recognize the kind of influence that reached one in the dream.

In these cases, we are not dealing with a pure dream, arising only from one's own bodily sensations but, rather, a person's ability to dream is being used by an external entity to present the sleeping person's consciousness with mental images from the outside, through the brain's ability to reflect them to the sleeper.

Upon awakening from dreams of this sort, most people are left with the feeling that this must have been something more than just a dream.

One instinctively senses the influence of the external source behind the dream.

The clarity of such a dream may be obscured, whether from one's own unsettled soul forces attempting to assert themselves or from the body's physical sensations inserting their own dream images.

Nevertheless, despite the interference, in many instances the actual message may still be discerned. This is because the intervening images emanating from one's own personal realm are altered to a greater or lesser degree if the transmission of external mental images is in progress at the time such personal images are being formed.

A sort of "translation" of the external mental images into symbolic dream experiences takes place, often difficult to interpret, yet often still recognizable as such.

The most famous example of such dream symbolism is found in the biblical narrative of the dream of the Egyptian pharaoh, that a young Hebrew slave was able to interpret.

If one takes this story as historical fact, even if only for example's sake, one can also assume that this pharaoh was not a total stranger to analytical thinking and that there existed among his wise men some who were expert in the art of interpreting dream symbols, an activity zealously pursued in ancient times.

The reason the pharaoh's own dream interpreters were unable to counsel him, while the Hebrew youth was able to explain the meaning of the dream quite clearly, is because the ability to interpret the symbolism of dreams can only be attained through intuition and not through formulaic thinking.

Since ancient times, folk superstition has embraced the interpretation of dreams and it cannot be denied that some of the rules of this vulgar form of dream interpretation are due to focusing exclusively on typically recurring dream symbols. When one examines the research of many dream investigators one can observe a pattern in the way dream insights become transformed into a corresponding series of mental images. At this point in time, however, those who wish to explore these relationships are likely to find themselves on very unstable ground and I strongly recommend leaving to rest those dreams that cannot be clearly and unequivocally explained.

The dreams that fit perfectly into this last category seldom occur.

Nonetheless, for those who know themselves to be sufficiently stable within so as to not unwittingly succumb to the oppression of foolish superstition, the analysis of their dreams and the interpretation of dream symbolism may prove to be of value.

There is nothing in our earthly life that cannot in some way or other be made to serve our spiritual life.

As with all other aspects of life, dreams only remain a mystery in as much as the underlying principles that govern them are not understood.

Those people who believe that their dream experiences represent an entrance into spiritual worlds—and there are still, even in our day, people inclined to such a view—mistake the path to delusion with the path to truth.

A person's spiritual body may indeed dwell on spiritual planes and gather experiences there while the physical body rests in deep sleep. However, only a pale reflection of these experiences is then translated into dream symbolism that reaches the earthly consciousness. These dream symbols are the means through which our own spiritual nature, of which we may still be unaware during waking life, tries to communicate to us its profound spiritual insights.

The act of consciously entering the spiritual realm with one's spiritual organism is different from any dream experience, no matter how sublime, and can only be achieved by those few beings on earth who have already been awake and active in these realms before donning the garment of the physical body.

This ability cannot be acquired through esoteric practice or strenuous discipline, except by those few chosen by the Primordial Light itself, so that they may act as bridge builders for their brothers and sisters imprisoned in the darkness of earthly perception.

A dream can nonetheless represent an image, a likeness of an experience that does not require use of the physical body, and yet, still actually takes place in a real organism and within real worlds.

Everything terrestrial, including dreams, can only be a shadowy reflection of spiritual Being.

Those who keep all this in mind as they seek to fathom the mystery of dreams may well gain insights both sacred and sublime.

CHAPTER FOUR

MANTIC ARTS

SINCE ANCIENT TIMES THE WORD "MANTIC" has referred to divination of all kinds, especially the prediction of coming events.

The ancients were acquainted with innumerable methods that they believed could foresee the future. Although these were mostly based on superstition, occasionally, in their zeal to reveal the future, the ancients were led to areas of significance beyond superstition.

Certain mantic arts have survived up to the present day and we are even witnessing a renewed interest in their practice.

Today it is not so much the desire to predict the future but, rather, an interest in the analysis of the psyche that inspires the practice of such arts.

To illustrate this point, let us consider an area of research referred to as graphology—although graphology is not, strictly speaking, one of the mantic arts. Graphology is actually a precise, scientific method of investigation and has become so accepted that even our state justice system routinely uses it for help.

A graphological analysis is very different indeed from the unveiling of the future.

Graphology is concerned with identifying people's character traits through the analysis of the unique and involuntary characteristics of their handwriting.

The interest in graphology is so great in all circles of society today that persons even moderately familiar with the basic tenets of this psychological research method must be very careful not to reveal their knowledge, in order to avoid being overwhelmed with countless requests for handwriting analysis.

From what I and others have been able to observe, the situation is similar with regard to the interest in the actual mantic arts that are still practiced today.

In most cases it is naive souls who either practice these arts themselves or consult one of their practitioners in order to find out something about the future. However, sometimes even those who are more sophisticated show an interest in such arts, particularly when they are concerned with the analysis of the psyche or of character.

The fact that the mantic arts are capable of analyzing a person's character and the attributes of the psyche is most clearly demonstrated by the practice of chiromancy. Chiromancy must be included among the mantic arts—as it has been historically—because it claims to also shed light on future events, not by means of calculation, as in astrology, but rather through the interpretation of the lines and marks of the hand.

It cannot be denied that the lines and fine runes of a hand are closely connected to a person's character. One need look no further for an explanation of why this is so if one keeps in mind that the stirrings of a person's psyche make themselves known through their effect on the finest nerve and muscle fibers.

One can, of course, say that a person's countenance reflects character better than the hand, since the face is far easier to interpret. It is true that most people will be able to gather more clues from a face than from a hand, however, the hand is still to be given preference here, since the possibility of fakery is far lower than is the case with facial expressions.

Many notorious scoundrels know how to worm themselves, through their "honest eyes," into somebody's confidence without having first earned it, whereas the lines of their hands would readily betray them to an expert.

The lines of the hand cannot be changed even through the most experienced dissimulation. Apart from the face, the hand is indisputably the part of the body most affected by a person's inner world.

Just as it is possible to pursue any endeavour in either an amateurish or a serious manner, it is also possible to analyze the runes of a hand in a serious manner or to just interpret them by rote and according to superficial rules.

It goes without saying that an intensive observation of many hands over a period of years is required in order to gain enough experience to achieve diagnostic certainty in this field.

Certain experiences from a person's past can be "read" from the traces that the psyche has left behind in the hands. Things become more complicated when chiromancy tries to predict future events.

A very proficient palm reader will be able to detect abilities and inclinations that can lead to particular future life experiences, unless their course is altered by the intervention of spiritual powers.

It is also possible to identify a person's purely physical disposition from the lines of the hand as well as the way events determined by physical habits will probably unfold throughout the phases of that person's life.

Both observations taken together make it possible to determine approximately when certain future events might occur. However, these predictions are always limited to a narrow sphere of psycho-physically determined possibilities.

Chiromancers who come up with accurate predictions beyond this sphere consciously or

unconsciously leave behind the field of chiromancy, even if they initially set out from it. In
reality their pronouncements are only par-
tially based on the observation of the lines of
the hand, while the most important information is actually transmitted through contact
with the subject's psyche. This contact comes
about spontaneously during the reading and
can lead to a kind of "clairsentience" in persons open to it.

Really proficient palm readers, whether they
are noted researchers in their field or simply
possessed of natural talents of which they
may be only partly aware, always owe their
ability to the coming together of all the above-
mentioned factors, and it is not possible to
draw precise lines of separation. The ability
to perceive underlying patterns coupled with
a knowledge of human nature may further im-
prove the result.

When outstanding results are achieved, it is
almost always because chiromancers gifted
with a strong intuition have made use of it in
combination with all of their other abilities.
One should bear in mind however, that this
intuitive ability should not be interpreted as
evidence of a higher spirituality, as it may

equally be found in those with ethically upright natures as well as completely corrupt
ones.

THE POWER OF INSPIRED intuition is perhaps the
single most important force in all the mantic
arts. When awakened, this force can convey
to even the simplest of human beings insights
impossible to gain by any scientific method.

Even learned researchers cannot attain satis-
factory results unless they learn to awaken the
intuitive powers slumbering within them, and
are able to listen to the voice of intuition despite the skepticism that their education and
training has instilled in them.

The experiences of countless people from all
walks of life have shown time and again how
through some mantic art astonishingly correct
results were obtained.

There are those who present themselves to the
world as being far above all "superstition,"
yet they secretly seek out every obscure back-
street Pythia, all too willing to believe the
testimonials of this or that person that she
"got it" all right.

It will not do here to hide one's head in the sand like an ostrich, so as to avoid seeing what one does not want to see.

Rather, it is important in all these cases to trace such abilities to their source—abilities that surface in all kinds of places and under all sorts of circumstances, some of them quite absurd—because the results are often noteworthy.

Asian fortune-tellers make use even today of certain small tablets or sticks with inscriptions thought to have magical qualities, which they cast while in a semi-conscious state, in order to answer questions posed to them. They then decipher the answers by interpreting patterns in the seemingly random combinations that result.

Similarly, in the temple sanctuaries of Tibetan monasteries one can find tablets that have the status of holy books, in that they are able to provide the answers to all questions that may be posed. However, their message can only be read by skilled persons, because they must be arranged and combined according to specific rules, if they are to reveal their secrets.

The tarot of the gypsies, ancestor of all card games, is very similar to these other practices.

Here too, the cards bearing symbolic signs, characters and images have to be laid out according to a specific method and following certain preparations, so that the answers to the questions asked can be read from the resulting combination. The "Madame card-reader" tucked away on the top floor of some run-down building, receiving a clientele who would otherwise never enter such places of poverty, has in most cases no clue as to the illustrious ancestry of the magical props she uses.

Nonetheless her work corresponds precisely with that of a Chinese fortune-teller, a Tibetan Lama, or an occultist of the caliber of Eliphas Lévis consulting the Tarot.

Similar causes lead to similar effects. It should be obvious, therefore, that underlying all these results, the same principles are at work. So the faithful of the major European cities swear just as much by the oracular pronouncements of their more or less questionable Sybils, as the people of the Dalai Lama do in the declarations of their priesthood.

Despite all the humbug that never lacks for its believers, and which one encounters in both eastern and western regions of this earth, results come to light that cannot be obtained through humbug, impressive enough to captivate skeptics and critics alike.

This is not surprising, since all the hocus-pocus that elicits such superstitious awe in the faithful, is actually a means through which fortune-tellers of all types create within themselves a state of concentration that allows them to make contact with the client's psyche.

It is this contact that makes it possible for fortune-tellers, depending on the strength of their intuitive abilities, to come up with results that produce such astonishment.

We human beings have hardly begun to realize how much more we could know about each other, if we understood how to connect with one another on the level of the psyche and to then listen to the voice of intuition.

Those who practice one of the mantic arts "professionally" quite naturally acquire the ability to create such psychic contact and with experience also develop insights into how to produce the necessary state of concentration. It is truly no wonder, then, when fortune-tellers tell their amazed clients things that they themselves have lost the ability to apprehend, as a result of their constant inner distraction.

What is truly amazing here is the degree of indifference with which most people simply permit the loss of their most wondrous abilities. They look quite foolish when, faced with seemingly impenetrable enigmas, some plain, uneducated person demonstrates the use of those very abilities. All mortals have the potential to make use of these abilities, were it not for the fact that they have become numbed to more subtle kinds of perception— regardless of how proud they may be of the "sureness" of their feelings.

MANY HAVE ASKED: Is it possible to reconcile the striving for higher spiritual development with the use of the mantic arts?

Here I can only respond that: "All things work together for good to them that love God."

All persons must decide for themselves if they prefer to have the direction of their lives determined by the predictions of fortune-tellers or if their self-respect allows them to secretly consult clairvoyants and card-readers. In reality, such curiosity is nothing other than a foolish weakness, and indicates that this person could not have come very far on the path toward the Spirit. Those who pursue this path with perseverance will feel themselves quite capable of finding all the answers to their questions within themselves, and will feel uncomfortable even considering the possibility of consulting others.

In the face of ample, experiential evidence to be found among all peoples on earth, it would be foolish to doubt that, through the practice of mantic arts it is possible to reach a significant and spontaneous increase in sensitivity to subtle influences. However, it would be equally foolish if one were to accord the "magical" tools of the fortune-teller some sort of special, mysterious significance—except for their function as an aid to achieving a particular state of concentration and for stimulating intuition.

A far more desirable and dignified path is to achieve such concentration without the paraphernalia which seem to have become inseparable from the practice of the mantic arts and without having to stimulate one's intuition through such external and sometimes questionable methods. In addition, the practice of any mantic art, even if only for the sake of research, can use up the forces of the soul to such an extent that there is hardly any space left for spiritual development.

Those who have truly entered onto the path toward the Spirit will have no need whatsoever to turn to any kind of mantic art, regardless of the accurate results these arts may yield, because whatever they might discover through the mantic arts will be given to them spiritually in right measure, so that they may be able to continue sure-footed on their hallowed path.

They will seek to make the most of everything they meet in life, whether the road ahead is dark and the future uncertain, or if, instead, the path has been illuminated for them.

They will always be aware that all mantic arts, indeed, all serious forecasts of the future, are based solely on a natural sequence of physical events. However, those who have been "born anew" in Spirit will also be able to rely on the Spirit's sublime powers to serve them and to avert many an event that might otherwise come to pass.

❧

CHAPTER FIVE

HYPNOSIS

I DO NOT THINK I NEED TO EXPEND A LOT OF effort giving a detailed explanation of what is meant by "hypnosis" and how this abnormal state of will and consciousness control can be brought about.

Unfortunately, there is far too much experimentation going on in this area nowadays and the phenomenon of hypnosis is discussed widely and extensively in both scholarly publications as well as in the most questionable treatises.

In my opinion, one ought to be extremely careful when giving instructions about how to induce a hypnotic state. Even the mere description of the hypnotic state is not without risk.

Such descriptions do not have a positive effect. On the contrary, they stimulate one's curiosity and awaken, depending on how active or passive the person's disposition, the desire to either want to hypnotize or be hypnotized.

The assumption that a successful hypnotist must be blessed with some mysterious power is still prevalent in most of society. This notwithstanding the frequent assertion that everyone supposedly has the ability to hypnotize and that only the hypnotist's will power plays a decisive role. In reality, however, things are quite different.

First of all, not everyone can induce the hypnotic state, no matter how familiar they are with the techniques of hypnosis and even if they are able to focus their will with perfect concentration. Secondly, hypnosis is by no means a matter of one person's will binding another person's will.

There are some very good hypnotists who are quite weak-willed, virtually incapable of single-mindedly pursuing a particular intention, while very strong-willed persons are often easily induced into a hypnotic trance.

Rather, there are forces at work here that have very little to do with the will. And when I spoke above of "binding the will," this is not to be understood as if the will itself is weakened in any way.

In the normal state, the body's organs respond almost exclusively to a person's own will, and are only accessible to external impulses of will in a limited way, and only when one's own will is diverted. In the hypnotic state, however, the link between the bodily organs and a person's own will is severed to such an extent that hypnotic subjects become unable to perceive their own will or, in less severe cases, are only able to respond to it very incompletely.

Hypnosis therefore is simply the process of progressively deepening the detachment of the will of a person from their brain.

The will is only able to transmit its impulses to the brain via subtle, fluidic forces of the material body, which form part of the unseen realm of the physical world. The hypnotic state is brought about by nothing more than the numbing of these subtle, fluidic forces.

While this paralysis is set in motion by the will of the hypnotist, the rest of the process does not depend on the strength of this impulse nor does it depend on which theory the hypnotist uses to explain the hypnotic state.

It is not actually the hypnotist who brings about the hypnotic state, although it certainly appears as if this is the case. And while the hypnotist's concentration is steadily held, it need not be of more than normal strength.

THE MANIFESTATIONS of hypnosis are based on a kind of "infection," as strange as this may sound when one considers the prevailing theories on the topic. In this case, we are not talking about a disease that is transmitted by germs and microbes. Rather, centers of energy, invisible to even the best microscope, cause a paralysis of the subtle, fluidic bodily forces, as a result of which these energy centers are able to directly act upon the brain, while at the same time deactivating the will of the person.

Hypnotists are persons whose psycho-physical constitution is particularly suited to stimulating such centers of energy so that they are impelled to respond to the hypnotists' wishes and to automatically carry out the task that is desired.

Not everybody is therefore able to hypnotize, just as not every person will be successful as a spiritistic "medium," even though in both cases these abilities are present to a certain degree in every human being.

The myriad, invisible centers of energy exist at every point of the unseen physical world and fill all space as a homogeneous mass. They only require an impulse of will to become "charged"—to become the active servant of that will—so that it almost appears as if one were dealing with minute, invisible, half-conscious beings.

It is not the hypnotist's impulse of will alone that forces them into action. Every desire, no matter how secret, activates them also, once such a desire succeeds in forcing the will to become its servant.

In the majority of human beings the subtle, fluidic bodily forces are insulated from external influence. Although in these instances there still can be some minor infiltration by the energy centers, their influence will always be minimal. However, one may also often come across a type of person whose own subtle, fluidic bodily forces have all but merged with these energy centers. Persons with this kind of psycho-physical constitution are, depending on whether their disposition is more active or more passive, either born hypnotists or born spiritistic "mediums."

Spiritistic mediumship also depends upon the forces of these invisible centers of energy. The medium passively surrenders to the influence of these energy centers, and is "hypnotized" by them. Thus, the true "hypnotist" here is to be found in the invisible realm of the physical world. In the case of one person hypnotizing another, it is a visible person who actively intervenes and artificially turns the subject—who may not have the natural disposition for this—into temporarily acting as a medium.

The whole process of hypnosis is essentially nothing other than what is generally referred to as "spiritism." Hypnosis differs from spiritism only insofar as during hypnosis actual persons influence one another, while during a spiritistic session the human hypnotist is replaced by an entity from the unseen realm of the physical world.

Even though a spiritistic trance may look quite different from a hypnotic state, they are nonetheless identical in essence. These states are produced with the help of the same forces, even if the precipitating factors are of a very different nature: on the one hand it is the impulse of a human being, while on the other it is the animal-like instinct of a lemuric entity from the unseen part of the physical world.

If all the hidden connections within nature were as evident to hypnotists as they are to the lemuric entities, hypnotists would be able to produce many of the "miracles" of spiritism, if they so desired, with the help of their hypnotic subjects. The only spiritistic phenomena they would be unable to produce are those for which a real medium is necessary under all circumstances. As mentioned above, the medium represents the passive type, and the hypnotist the active type, of the same kind of psycho-physical constitution.

A person hypnotizing another person, however, can apprehend only that part of nature that can be perceived through the physical senses. Because of this limitation, such a person is not capable of realizing that the invisible entities of the physical world have temporarily taken possession of the hypnotized person who, in this way, has been artificially turned into a "medium"—and is also not able to prevent this from happening.

For this reason, it is possible for some people to seriously believe that, in the deeper hypnotic states, one is in touch with a person's spiritual nature—to trust that one is being instructed by a transpersonal level of the subconscious. None of these people ever suspect that they in fact are holding spiritistic séances, bowing respectfully to revelations issuing from the same sphere as everything the "dear spirits" of some spiritistic circle tell their devout friends. These twilight entities have the uncanny ability to strike just the right note, artfully tailored to the sensibilities of their listeners, so that their "messages from the beyond" will be believed.

ALTHOUGH HYPNOSIS was initially branded as fraud and superstition, it has nowadays become an indispensable tool of medical practice, and has been credited with many a successful cure.

It is not my task to assess the extent to which these therapeutic successes will hold up under scrutiny and withstand the test of time.

However, I must state frankly, that all healing with the help of hypnosis is roughly equivalent to the expulsion of the Devil through Beelzebub and may pose the same dangers for the practicing physician as it does for the patient.

One must earnestly ask whether the benefits of actual or presumed healing successes outweigh the risks of courting such dangers.

This decision I leave to the judgment of medical practitioners, while here I only want to point out the nature of the dangers that threaten.

Anyone who studies spiritism more closely, whether through personal observation or through the relevant literature, should be well aware that mediums fall into a trance more easily the more they experiment with such states.

Hypnotists have this same experience with their subjects, who fall more easily into a hypnotic state the more they are hypnotized.

The energy centers causing the abnormal state in both medium and hypnotic subject are permanently "tuned," so to speak, to achieving this state in the person concerned; they form a kind of magic chain, continually connecting the active with the passive pole.

This connection takes place is the unseen part of the physical world, the sphere to which those fine fluidic forces of the body also belong. When activated, it is these forces that trigger autonomous impulses of will in the brain; when anesthetized, one's sovereign sense of self is pushed from its throne and forced to surrender to some other power, which then is able to manipulate the brain as it pleases.

The more a hypnotist experiments with a subject, the more a doctor uses hypnosis with a patient, the more indissoluble the magic chain of invisible energy centers connecting both poles becomes, even if thousands of miles should separate one from the other.

This magic chain is almost infinitely stretchable and is less likely to tear, the more it has been tempered through numerous hypnotic experiments.

As a result of such a permanent connection the doctor or the hypnotist, as well as the patient or the subject, may experience some very unpleasant influences. This is because the relationship between the poles is not so rigidly fixed that it may not be possible at times for the active pole to become passive and vice versa.

In only a minute number of cases will such unwanted mutual influence be recognized as such, notwithstanding the fact that reliable observations have on occasion been made that can only be explained through such a permanent fluidic connection.

Certain secret schools of the occult avail themselves deliberately of this possibility for manipulation. The "teachers" concerned "instruct" their victims in sessions that in reality are nothing other than a continuously intensifying series of more-or-less disguised hypnotic anesthetizations, gradually binding their victims to such an extent that they are hardly in command of their own will any longer.

Such occultist adventurers know full well that all their power would be at stake were they to let go, even for the shortest period of time, of their active role, to which they cling with such single-minded determination. They will hardly be in danger of experiencing disagreeable incursions from their so effectively fettered "students."

Physicians, however, whose active role is limited to the duration of the hypnotic session, are never safe from unexpected intrusions of their patients' will into their own psychophysical being, into their own thoughts and feelings—even if they have long since forgotten about the patient.

The fact that patients are affected to a far greater extent in this way, lies in the nature of the agreed-upon relationship.

More important than all the technical dangers of which most professional hypnotists are aware, however, is the incontrovertible fact that every hypnotic anesthetization, whether undertaken for experimental or for healing purposes, creates a barrier between the will and the brain of the hypnotized person. In persons who have been hypnotized many times, the after-effects of this separation of will from brain gradually extend far beyond the duration of the hypnotic session.

I am not referring here to post-hypnotic suggestion, in which the subject falls automatically into a state of hypnosis after a specified time period has elapsed and carries out the will of the hypnotist exactly as if the original hypnotic session were still in progress. This happens because the subject's fine fluidic bodily forces, which enable the will to direct the brain, have been impressed by the hypnotist with an instruction that the hypnotic suggestion will be acted upon after the lapse of a specified period of time.

I also do not mean the inhibition of the will for therapeutic reasons. In these cases the hypnotized patients, having returned to the waking state, still find themselves restrained, for a long time, from giving in to certain desires, harboring certain fears or the like. These are all after-effects desired by the hypnotist which are, strictly speaking, phenomena of the actual session, even if they manifest at a later stage.

After-effects of a far more serious nature arise in frequently hypnotized persons in the form of damage intended by neither side. Persons who become accustomed to passively allowing others to do with them as they please, gradually lose their ability to resist the influence of an outside will or the pressure from external suggestions.

When hypnotists command their subjects, with the best of intentions, to be impervious to the influence of anyone other than the hypnotist, this does not help in the least.

As a result of such suggestive commands, subjects do indeed become highly resistant to hypnotic anesthetization from anyone else, however, during daily life, as a result of the constant inhibition of their own will, they become incapable of staying in complete control of their brain.

The brain then becomes a playground for every imaginable foreign impulse of will.

Surely, no one with any degree of insight into these matters would ever assert that such a state could be considered desirable for a person's higher spiritual development.

Moreover, when hypnosis is used for therapeutic reasons, it focuses primarily on the suppression of certain constitutional defects that actually belong to the moral sphere.

When one achieves this control by virtue of one's own will power, even if only after many failed attempts and after long intervals of time, the result may be considered a truly positive gain for the entire inner life of the person.

Through this process, the will gradually acquires complete dominion over the brain, so that unwanted foreign influences, or even undesired impulses arising from within one's own constitution, become less and less able to overpower it.

If, on the other hand, one strives to eliminate such defects through the use of hypnosis, one may indeed succeed in making the undesired characteristic disappear, but by no means has the development of the soul been advanced. The power of the will over the brain, without which no true perfection of the soul would ever be possible on this earth, is thereby eroded more and more.

FROM EVERYTHING I have put forward here, although I have not gone into detail, it should be evident that involvement with hypnosis is a very questionable game, fraught with as many dangers as the practice of spiritistic mediumship or efforts to learn certain fakir arts.

The phenomenon of hypnosis should give even superficial souls cause for serious thought regarding the mysterious regions within which the inner life of a human being unfolds.

Such cautionary knowledge can contribute to shaping our view of the world, and thus be of great value to every individual. Hypnosis and related phenomena can never be a blessing to humanity and do not in truth help reveal to us the mystery of our own existence.

⚭

CHAPTER SIX

ENIGMAS OF THE FUTURE

THE DESIRE TO KNOW THE FUTURE AND TO see coming events with our inner eye is as old as humanity itself. And yet, not a single human being on this planet has been able to part the dense, dark curtain behind which the future lies.

But, you may ask, have not all peoples of this planet had their prophets? Have we not heard countless, ancient tidings from seers who knew the future's secrets? Has not Nostradamus's *The Centuries* gained renewed recognition in our day?

None of this is unfamiliar to me and yet I must unfortunately state that in no other matter has humanity so stubbornly deceived itself as in the faith that it is possible to fully foretell the future.

True, there have always been some individuals to whom future events have on occasion been unveiled and that such people can be found among us in the present time and will be in times to come.

This is so because the future is contained in the present, just as the present is only the product of the past.

Such unveiling may be brought about in a variety of ways.

The radiant forces from the realm of pure Spirit as well as the practice of the mantic arts are able to awaken, for moments, an intuitive knowledge of the future. Still, only fragments of future events ever reveal themselves thus to the seer, and then only in shadowy and symbolic imagery.

Seers of the future are never masters of the images they see.

Those images will likely contain things they do not want to see, and that which they deeply desire to behold, will remain hidden.

They must accept the images as they appear and understand that they cannot change the form in which the images present themselves:

sometimes with straightforward clarity and precision, at other times in a phantasmagorical and arabesque-like manner.

The seer is only the recipient of tidings from afar, not the discoverer of unexplored lands.

I⊤ SHOULD BE APPARENT that I am speaking here of prophetic seeing and not of the methods with which hidden science is able to calculate the ebb and flow of coming times—although today such methods are still imperfect.

The result will not differ substantially no matter which approach one uses for such calculations: whether one analyzes the position of the earth respective to the cosmos, or if one creates a scheme from the known data about terrestrial events—a kind of calculation-web into which future events can then be woven.

As imperfect as these methods are, they nevertheless are the only reasonably precise means we have of predicting future events, analagous to the way today's meteorologists are able to predict many climatic events by measuring atmospheric pressure at different locations around the globe. Here too, errors will be unavoidable until, through experience, we gain a better understanding of the laws that govern the unfolding of natural phenomena.

Such future calculations will also have their limits but, within those limits, much can be explored with relative confidence, and will be of more use to humanity than any oracle-like visions of the future, over which the seer has no control. Such calculations, although they certainly have value, are not needed for higher insight.

THE IDEA THAT ALL terrestrial time is revealed to the eye of an eternal presence is presumptuous and the product of misguided speculation.

From this idea a bizarre theoretical construct arose, which explains time as being akin to a roll of film that one can simply unwind in order to come across desired images of the future.

This arrogant and conceited thinking has spun out a spider's web of pseudo-wisdom and caught a swarm of dayflies attracted to the nightlight of this intellectual delusion—so that now anyone who does not join in the delusion is looked down on with condescending pity.

Inexorable reality however, is not concerned with intellectual speculation or wild, super-stitious fantasies.

Reality is grounded only in itself and defies all theories that attempt to explain it.

Those who lack the courage to face reality eye to eye, and allow themselves to be deceived by dazzling doctrines, will forever have their thoughts tethered to the puppet strings of error.

Even though the most distant future is con-tained within the present, it is not yet visible to the eternal eye. The future becomes visible only as it unfolds.

All things that exist are merely the expression of underlying, creative energies, and since the future, too, is created by these energies, it can only be comprehended by the con-sciousness once it comes into existence. This explains why prophecy sees coming events as images appearing to already exist in some other dimension.

The nature of prophetic seeing has given rise to the mistaken view that the future is nothing other than an "eternal present," and simplistic thinking has sought ways to build a foundation for this fallacy.

HUMAN MINDS FIND it difficult not to think in anthropomorphic terms. Hence, the idea took hold that there must exist some sort of planetary guidance that knows what will happen at every moment and even into the farthest reaches of the future.

Humanity has been incapable of ascending to the snowy heights of Reality in order to distinguish, from that unobstructed view, between truth and delusion.

Planetary guidance truly does exist, but it differs very much from the mistaken mental construct created by baseless speculation.

The state that one might call "cosmic consciousness" is really only ever the living consciousness of the present moment—the present that is the sum of the myriad moments that have gone before and the creator of all the myriad moments to come.

"The spirit searches everything, even the depths of God." Thus, it is indeed possible for the spirit to unveil coming events through calculation and inference, and through the insights of profound meditation, in which the spirit becomes aware of its own inherent laws. However, only spirits quite remote from God still yearn for such knowledge. Supreme Reality, recognizing itself in itself as primordial light, as the origin of all that is and the crown of all existence—comprehending itself through all eternity only as Being fully conscious in the present moment—knows no urge to search the past, nor to destroy the absolute harmony of cosmic reality that the present moment offers, through knowledge of things to come.

Pay heed, whoever is willing to hear my words! Many false conclusions have been drawn from erroneous assumptions about "god" and the "divine." A mental image of spiritual reality has been planted in our minds, so that, through this image, the divine might be worshipped as an idol, or quarrelled with when it proves to be powerless, or even stripped of its glory.

Only when this image, which was created in order to inspire worship, is destroyed for all time, will the Living God be able to speak to humanity again.

Then will humanity also learn to live fully in the present moment and any urge to know the future will vanish.

LIVING IN THE PRESENT moment lifts humanity into life's divine dimension.

The myriad moments that form our earthly life then line up like precious pearls on a string until one day, in life eternal, we find ourselves in the constant same moment that encompasses the experience of the eternal—the jewel in the thousand-petalled lotus blossom.

OM MANI PADME HUM!

REMINDER

"Yet here I must point out again that if one would derive the fullest benefit from studying the books I wrote to show the way into the Spirit, one has to read them in the original; even if this should require learning German.

"Translations can at best provide assistance in helping readers gradually perceive, even through the spirit of a different language, what I convey with the resources of my mother tongue."

From "Answers to Everyone" (1933), *Gleanings*. Bern: Kobersche Verlagsbuchhandlung, 1990

For a deeper understanding
of the core of Bô Yin Râ's teachings
you may want to read:

The Book on the Living God,
The Book on Life Beyond and
The Book on Human Nature

These three books should be
read together.

A description of all three books follows.

THE BOOK ON THE LIVING GOD

The Book on the Living God describes the inner path that leads to birth of the Living God within—what we must do and what to avoid on the long journey towards awakening the consciousness of our timeless self.

Ordinary consciousness, Bô Yin Râ tells us, is actually like sleep; there is a greater consciousness that is alive in us, informing every cell, and our task is to unite it with our self-awareness. He reassures us that we are not alone on this journey; there are helpers here on earth who give us inner support and act as transformers, enabling us to receive needed spiritual energies that would otherwise be too powerful to tolerate.

Bô Yin Râ recommends practices to help us on the path: He counsels us to set aside time for daily contemplation and to meditate on words that touch and uplift us. Words in particular can be a gateway to an expanded sense of existence, because they embody hidden energies. The key is to experience their aliveness and not just understand them mentally. We should strive to master and unify the many thoughts and wills that struggle within us and cultivate an attitude of quiet joy and serene detachment.

We must also set aside the ideas we have been taught about an anthropomorphic God. God is not meant to be an external object of worship but, rather, an experience to be awakened within us. We are cautioned to avoid the pitfalls that might divert us: following false teachers or believing that certain foods or exercises, or ecstatic experiences have spiritual merit. Everyday life, when lived with attention to the ultimate goal, will lead us towards a gradual awakening of our timeless self.

E.W.S. Publisher

Contents: Word of Guidance. "The Tabernacle of God is with Men." The White Lodge. Meta-Physical Experiences. The Inner Journey. The En-Sof. On Seeking God. On Leading an Active Life. On "Holy Men" and "Sinners." The Hidden Side of Nature. The Secret Temple. Karma. War and Peace. The Unity among Religions. The Will to Find Eternal Light. The Human Being's Higher Faculties of Knowing. On Death. On the Spirit's Radiant Substance. The Path toward Perfection. On Everlasting Life. The Spirit's Light Dwells in the East. Faith, Talismans, and Images of God. The Inner Force in Words. A Call from Himavat. Giving Thanks. Epilogue.

THE BOOK ON LIFE BEYOND

The Book on Life Beyond is a guide to help readers understand what they can expect to find in the life beyond death, and how to best prepare for it.

Bô Yin Râ explains that life beyond is actually another dimension of the same life we know here on earth—just as real and solid, but perceived through spiritual, rather than our limited, physical senses. He emphasizes the direct connection between our actions here on earth and their effects on life beyond. We bring with us into life beyond the same state of inner being with which we departed, and are able to experience its wonders exactly to the degree to which we have developed our spiritual self. For example, those who have failed to show compassion for others and have lived selfishly will find that life beyond lacks the warmth and light that other, more developed souls can perceive.

Bô Yin Râ counsels us to mentally practice the "art of dying" as a meditative practice to prepare for the transition from physical to spiritual existence. The goal is to constantly orient one's thinking, emotions and desires toward transformation of the self, in order to be able to receive the spiritual help that will be available to us after death.

E.W.S. Publisher

Contents: Introduction. The Art of Dying. The Temple of Eternity and the World of Spirit. The Only Absolute Reality. What Should One Do?

THE BOOK ON HUMAN NATURE

The Book on Human Nature presents basic concepts about human nature with the goal of inspiring readers to awaken the timeless, spiritual spark within. We become fully human only when the spiritual potential within us gradually awakens and infuses our material, purely animal selves. It is a path that every human being may and should pursue.

A central understanding is that all life results from the joining of opposites, in particular, the polarity of male and female energies. Bô Yin Râ emphasizes that the true spiritual human being is male and female united in one entity; when we seek our spiritual self, we must call forth the male and female in ourselves and in all things. He discusses the biblical fall from grace as a descent from the spiritual plane, in which male and female were united, onto a material plane, in which male and female are split apart.

Bô Yin Râ warns men that holding onto the illusion of male superiority means forfeiting their spiritual life. While the spiritual paths that are natural for men and women are different in tone—open and receptive for women, active and grasping for men—they are equal and complementary. He tells us that *true* marriage is preparation for the life beyond: by coordinating the desires, wills and attitudes of two beings we once again bring about, in some measure, the original state in which male and female energies are united.

E.W.S. Publisher

Contents: Introduction. The Mystery Enshrouding Male and Female. The Path of the Female. The Path of the Male. Marriage. Children. The Human Being of the Age to Come. Epilogue. A Final Word.

THE KOBER PRESS